Basic Skills

Summarizing

Focusing on Main Ideas and Details and Restating in Concise Form

Grades 3-4

By
Cindy Karwowski

Cover Artist
Laura Zarrin

Inside Illustrations by
Rebecca Waske

Published by Instructional Fair • TS Denison
an imprint of

 **McGraw-Hill**
Children's Publishing

About the Author

Cindy Karwowski completed her bachelor's degree at Carthage College in Kenosha, Wisconsin. She earned her master's degree in elementary education at Michigan State University. She has taught elementary school for thirty years, ranging from grades one through four. Cindy has twice been a finalist for Michigan Teacher of the Year. She has been involved in many educational committees and has written several books for McGraw-Hill Children's Publishing.

Credits

Author: Cindy Karwowski

Cover Artist: Laura Zarrin

Cover Design: Matthew Van Zomeren

Inside Illustrations: Rebecca Waske

Project Director/Editor: Mary Hassinger

Editors: Sara Bierling, Alyson Kieda

Graphic Layout: Tracy L. Wesorick

McGraw-Hill
Children's Publishing

A Division of The McGraw-Hill Companies

Published by Instructional Fair • TS Denison
An imprint of McGraw-Hill Children's Publishing
Copyright © 2001 McGraw-Hill Children's Publishing

Send all inquiries to:
McGraw-Hill Children's Publishing
3195 Wilson Drive NW
Grand Rapids, Michigan 49544

Summarizing—grades 3-4
ISBN: 0-7424-0106-5

2 3 4 5 6 7 8 9 RPI 07 06 05 04 03 02

About the Book

Summarizing is the skill of comprehending, focusing on important information, and rephrasing the information in a concise form. *Summarizing 1–2* contains guided activities that help develop and achieve this skill. Students will progress from selecting main ideas and details to writing their own summaries. As this skill is practiced in reading, students will naturally begin to use the skill in writing and speaking. Summarization is a concept used throughout the curriculum. Social studies, science, language, and reading all use the skill of summarization in written, read, and oral lessons.

This book is especially designed to help practice the concept of summarization by modeling examples of summaries and providing practice in pinpointing important events in stories, poems, and cartoons.

Table of Contents

Clever Boy, Wise Mom

Complete the story's summary by writing the number of the picture that best fits the meaning of each sentence. Some numbers may be used more than once.

One day Jimmy raced into the kitchen and announced, "I am no longer eating anything green! I just found out that all green food was developed to turn humans into aliens. So I won't be able to eat anything like peas or broccoli! Besides, I'm sure that Mr. Johnson would not allow me to stay in class if I suddenly became an alien." Jimmy, who had always been a fussy eater, grinned as he watched his mom's stunned expression.

"I'm so sorry to hear that, Jimmy," replied his mom. I guess that you won't be having any pistachio cupcakes or lime sherbet for dessert tonight." This time his mom's face beamed as she observed her son's stunned expression.

A little _____ did not like eating _____ vegetables

so he invented a _____ about how eating _____ food would

turn him into an _____. He _____ at his own cleverness.

However, his mom ruined his plan by serving _____

_____ for dessert. She _____ at how she had fooled him.

1	2	3
4	5	6

IF5641 Summarizing

"Chews"ing a Dentist

Name _____

Write the correct word on each line to complete the summary of the cartoon strip. Some words may be used more than once.

A _____ visited a _____ because her close

_____ needed his teeth _____. Because he had dental

_____ and Dr. Kay Nine's _____ were fair, the

_____ made an _____. At 1:00 pm, the _____

and her friend, the _____, arrived for the _____.

Word Bank

friend	charges	dentist	appointment
insurance	alligator	zookeeper	cleaned

Harry

I have a special pet.
I love him very much.
He's got silky, smooth hair
That I always love to touch.

His fur is blackish brown—
But combing's not necessary.
He loves his tummy rubbed.
He is my best friend Harry.

Harry's not your average pet.
He weighs 100 pounds!
He's usually very quiet
Except for gurgling sounds.

Harry likes webs,
But not computer sites.
He's always on the move.
He likes to scale great heights.

Sometimes I ride his back.
I hold onto him so tight.
His eight legs travel so fast
That soon we're outta-sight!

1. Check the sentence that best summarizes Harry.
   a._____ Harry's strong body and legs let him climb high and run quickly.
   b._____ Harry probably grew so large by eating massive bugs.
   c._____ Harry is very proud of his powerful body and wonderful fur.

2. Check the sentence that best summarizes the speaker.
   a._____ The speaker always collected spiders but is especially proud of Harry.
   b._____ The speaker found Harry when he was very young and fed him a special diet, so he would grow very large.
   c._____ The speaker loves Harry very much, is proud of him, and really enjoys being with him.

3. Check the sentence that best summarizes the entire poem.
   a._____ The speaker's special pet has beautiful fur and is soft and cuddly.
   b._____ The speaker loves his special pet Harry, an oversized spider.
   c._____ Harry is the world's largest spider.

A Birthday Surprise!

Carefully study the cartoon. Fill in the blanks to complete a summary of the picture.

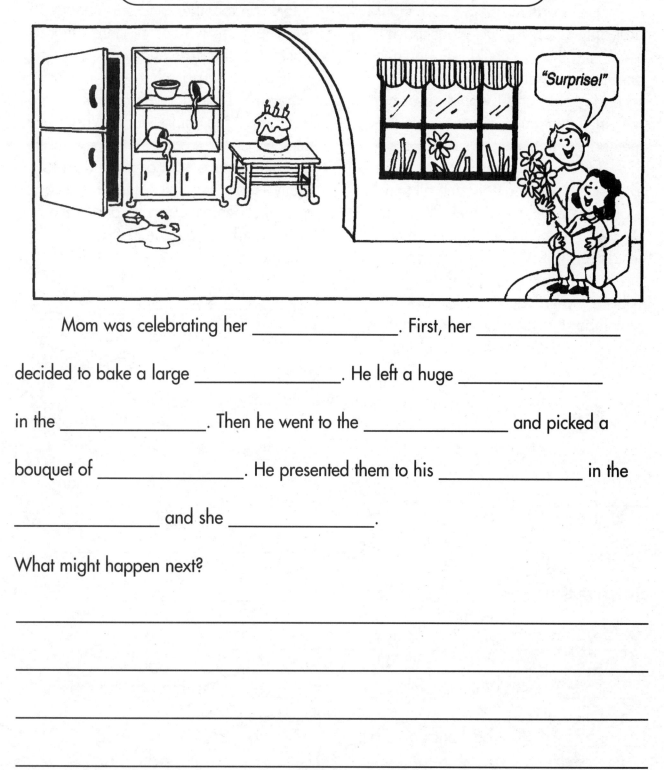

Mom was celebrating her _____. First, her _____

decided to bake a large _____. He left a huge _____

in the _____. Then he went to the _____ and picked a

bouquet of _____. He presented them to his _____ in the

_____ and she _____.

What might happen next?

_____

_____

_____

_____

  IF5641 Summarizing

Mayra's Backpack Attack

Read the paragraphs carefully and complete the exercise.

School starts tomorrow, so I should probably empty my lucky backpack. Mom said that we could buy another one, but I've had this backpack since second grade, and I would never part with it! It contains too many special memories! Hmmmm, let's see. Here's that 100% spelling test I got in October. It was the only one all year! Oooh! Here's that one with 30% that Dad was supposed to sign. I lost a recess for that. Wow! I forgot about this cool, hopping frog that even "ribbits" when you touch its back. I remember this artwork. I was painting a beautiful butterfly when all of the colors ran together, and so I changed it to a big, brown beetle. Here's that stack of flash cards and Laurie's stuffed monkey. I'll surprise her with it tomorrow. I love this ten-color pen. Too bad only three colors work. What's this? A bunch of candy wrappers, half a cookie, and a stick of gum. It looks pretty empty now except for this sticky, gooey, chocolate cupcake and melted ice cream bar from the last day of school.

"Hey, Mom, maybe I should get a new backpack after all!"

Unscramble the letters to complete a summary of the story.

School was starting, so _____ wanted to clean her lucky
ayMra

_____. Inside she found many things like _____ tests, a hop-
kkaaccbp   lsinpegl

ping _____, a painting of a _____, _____
grfo   eeebtl   shfal

cards, a stuffed _____, a ten-color _____,
ykoenm   epn

_____ wrappers, half a _____, and a stick of
ncayd   okcoei

_____. When she felt a _____ mess, she decided she needed
ugm   ckitsy

a _____ backpack after all.
wen

Vroo-o-o-m!

Use the information in the cartoon strip to fill in the blanks.

Main Story Details = introduction, important details, conclusion

Axle Rod Jones is building a special _____. First, he fastens on the

_____ _____ . Then he bolts on four _____ .

Finally, he ties on some _____ . Axle Rod Jones creates a car that travels

over _____ by rolling over a _____ .

Minor Story Details = unnecessary details but add interest

Axle's nickname is _____ . The special tires can _____ .

Axle's friend _____ when he realizes he has been tricked.

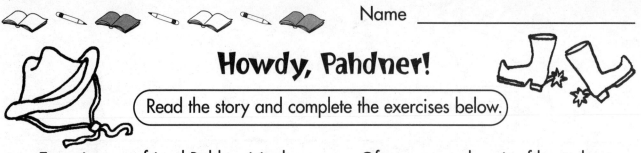

Howdy, Pahdner!

Read the story and complete the exercises below.

Ever since my friend Bobby visited a horse ranch, he has become a different person. We can't even call him Bobby anymore. He has informed us that his new name is Buck.

The only kind of shoes Buck wears now are boots! His favorite powder blue boots match the blue sky on the open range, Buck says. Buck's even talking about adding in-line wheels to a pair of boots. He told me that he even sleeps in boots, so he can go to bed with his shoes on—just like the horse that he rode out West.

Of course, each pair of boots has a coordinating shirt and hat.

I thought this cowboy thing was just a phase of Buck's life that would only last a few weeks. Now I think that this is more than a phase. Yesterday, Buck attached a toy horse head and tail to his mountain bike. He claimed that it would give him additional "horsepower."

I am convinced Buck is not just "horsing around." Buck may actually become a cowboy when he grows up!

1. Check the sentence that best summarizes Buck.
   a._____ Buck cares greatly about what his friends think of him and wants to please them with his actions.
   b._____ Buck has viewed numerous cowboy movies, and this has influenced his choice of a future career.
   c._____ Buck has become infatuated with many aspects of being a cowboy and has woven that into his life.

2. Check the sentence that best summarizes Buck's friend.
   a._____ His friend feels that Buck is overzealous in acting like a cowboy.
   b._____ His friend considers Buck's actions normal for a boy his age.
   c._____ His friend thinks Buck's cowboy clothing and style are cool.

3. Check the sentence that best summarizes the entire story.
   a._____ Buck loves all aspects of being a cowboy, and his friend is very jealous.
   b._____ Buck has become totally engrossed in acting like a cowboy, and his friend is concerned about him.
   c._____ Buck enjoys what he learned at the ranch. His friend wants to accompany him next year and become a cowboy, too.

IF5641 Summarizing

Name _____

Presto Chango!

Read the cartoon strip summary below. Cross off any sentences that contain unnecessary details for retelling the story.

A young magician performed magic tricks. She was called the Great Hoodwinker. First, she made a big, juicy apple disappear. It looked big and juicy. She ate it. Next, she announced that some tacks would float up into the air. She used a magnet to lift them up. It was a large, horseshoe magnet. Last, she pulled a hair from her magic hat. The audience probably thought she meant "hare" as in "rabbit."

1. Check the sentence that best summarizes the entire cartoon strip.

   a. _____ The Great Hoodwinker is an excellent magician.

   b. _____ This magician fooled the audience by tricking them with the words she

   used.

   c. _____ It is difficult to understand how the Great Hoodwinker performs her

   tricks.

A Change in Attitude

Circle the verse that contains the introduction.
Box the verse that contains the conclusion.

Sometimes when I am very bored,
I close my eyes in bed.
Suddenly, I begin to change.
I'm something else instead!

First time I shut my eyes so tight
I dreamed of being big,
Not small and scrawny anymore.
I turned into a pig.

I liked the part of no more baths.
All day I rolled in mud,
But when I tried to run,
I'd fall down with a "thud!"

The second time began so fun,
I dreamed of being tall.
I thought I might be a giraffe.
Instead, I was a wall.

I was the tallest one around.
No one dared to call me "short,"
But when playing with the other kids,
It's no fun to be the fort!

The third time seemed to be just right.
I wanted to be cool,
But I would rather be a swimmer
Than the swimming pool!

The others dived off the board.
All I could do was splash.
With all the chlorine that was used,
I got a great green rash!

I thought I had the perfect wish,
But it soon became a pain.
I really wanted to be smart.
I changed into a brain!

I knew so many math facts.
Science was a cinch for me!
But life's worth more than that.
What a catastrophe!

I might be small and kind of short.
I may not pass each test.
But if I have pride in what I do,
I'll be my very best!

A Change in Attitude (cont.)

1. Number the following sentences in the correct order to form the poem's summary.

_____ Then he changed into a brain so he could feel smart.

_____ The boy learned that he should take pride in himself and do his best.

_____ The boy became a swimming pool.

_____ A boy found he could change himself whenever he was bored.

_____ Next, he turned into a wall so he could be tall.

_____ He became a pig so he could feel big.

Try This: With a partner, discuss three things you would like to change into. Tell why you'd wish to change.

A Surprise Guest

Carefully study the cartoon. Read the summaries below.
Circle the letter of the summary that best describes the cartoon.

a. Some campers become friends with a family of bears.
They share dinner together, and all play cards. Later,
they become frightened when a friendly dinosaur
wants to join in their fun.

b. The campers are getting ready for bed. Then some
frightened bears charge into the tent because a large
dinosaur begins eating from the same garbage can they
just visited.

c. A family of campers are playing cards. Suddenly,
several bears dash into the tent because a dinosaur
approached them while they were eating from a nearby
garbage can. Everyone in the tent is very worried when
they realize what is standing outside.

Breakfast of Winners

Underline one sentence from **Group 1** and one
sentence from **Group 2** to form a brief summary of the essay below.

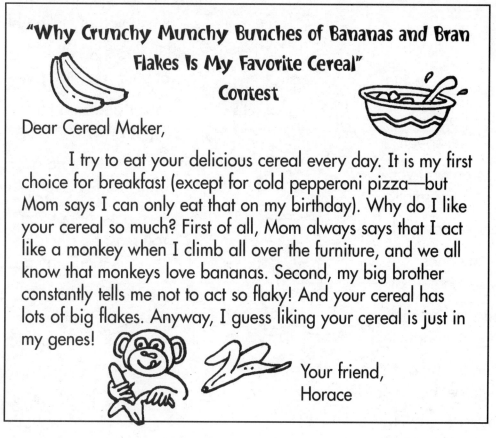

"Why Crunchy Munchy Bunches of Bananas and Bran Flakes Is My Favorite Cereal"
Contest

Dear Cereal Maker,

    I try to eat your delicious cereal every day. It is my first choice for breakfast (except for cold pepperoni pizza—but Mom says I can only eat that on my birthday). Why do I like your cereal so much? First of all, Mom always says that I act like a monkey when I climb all over the furniture, and we all know that monkeys love bananas. Second, my big brother constantly tells me not to act so flaky! And your cereal has lots of big flakes. Anyway, I guess liking your cereal is just in my genes!

    Your friend,
    Horace

Group 1

a. A child has entered a contest to determine which contestant eats the most of a particular type of cereal.

b. A child has entered a contest to determine which person has the best reasons for eating a particular brand of cereal.

c. A child has entered a contest to determine which cereal has the best crunch and munch qualities.

Group 2

a. He feels that his behaving like a monkey and acting a bit flaky should make him the winner.

b. He feels that Crunchy Munchy Bunches of Bananas and Bran Flakes has the best combination of fruit and corn flakes.

c. He feels that he eats their cereal most because he has it every day of the year except for his birthday.

Choosing Friends Wisely

Complete the song's summary by circling the correct word in each sentence.

—Sung to the tune of "Rock-a-Bye Baby."

Haven't you ever met Vanity Pride?

Sometimes she's present;
    sometimes she'll hide.

When she appears,
    you feel so tall

That others around you
    seem very small.

With her you may wish to speak,,

Tease the shy ones,
    make them weak—

Make them feel smaller
    than they now feel.

They'll look up to you;
    you'll be their ideal!

Vanity causes trouble for you.

She often comes out
    when you're feeling blue.

"You're better than all
    of your friends," she'll say.

"Find cooler and smarter friends
    right away!"

Vanity Pride will not go away
    Until you learn kind things to say

'Bout ev'ry person that you will meet
    You must be sincere
        without any deceit.

That's the lesson of Vanity Pride.
    A secret about her
        I'll now confide.

To get rid of her; to say, "Good-bye!"

Just eat a huge helping
    of humble pie!

When Vanity Pride appears, she often makes us act _____ **kind / cruel** to others. She convinces us that we are _____ **worse / better** than our friends. Vanity sometimes builds up our _____ **confidence / ability** so greatly that we destroy others' faith in themselves. If you wish for her to leave, you should become more _____ **proud / humble** and speak and act nicely to everyone.

IF5641 *Summarizing*

Whodunit?

> Write the story's summary by rewriting the sentences below
> in the correct order. Use a separate sheet of paper.

I heard Mom scream, "The pineapple upside-down cake I just baked for the school's Open House is half-eaten! Who could have done this?"

Mom needed my help. I studied the room carefully for clues. Suddenly, I slipped on a big pile of cake crumbs. I wiped off my pants and followed the crumbs into the living room where the trail abruptly ended. There, sitting and looking innocent, were Dad, little Jake, and Biscuit, our dog. They tried to ignore me by watching T.V. and eating popcorn. I decided that they would all remain suspects until the thief was caught. I circled each one slowly, examining for crumbs. Each seemed clean except for an occasional misplaced kernel of popcorn. I was totally baffled! The cake couldn't have vanished into thin air!

Then I looked up and noticed the door to Pollyanna's cage was open! She was perched atop our artificial palm tree. In her best parrot voice, Pollyanna announced, "Aloha ... Mmmmmm!" Aloha means "hello or good-bye" in Hawaiian, and we all know what *mmmmmm* means. The case was solved!

Pollyanna said, "Aloha," a Hawaiian word.

Since pineapples are grown in Hawaii, I concluded that the parrot had eaten the cake.

I carefully checked my dad, little brother, and dog for crumbs.

The parrot's cage was open.

I followed cake crumbs from the kitchen to the living room.

Mom yelled from the kitchen that her cake was half-eaten.

Little Rhett Riding's Hood

Carefully read this new version of an old story.

Grandma was feeling a bit "under the weather." The day before she had been skating in the annual "Gray Grannies Glide for Glory Marathon" when she missed a curve, flew ten feet in the air, and landed in the middle of Poindexter's Pond. Besides both her bottom and her ego being bruised, she caught a horrendous cold. Her granddaughter, Rhett Riding, happened to see the event on the nightly news and decided to bring her grandmother a heating pad, some cold medicine, and a plateful of her favorite chocolate, peanut butter cookies. Like Superman, she flung on her crimson cape (which she only wore in emergency situations) and proceeded to walk to her grandmother's house.

On the way, little Rhett (as she preferred to be called) came face-to-face with a very nosey wolf who asked her numerous questions about her day's activities. Rhett responded each time with a curt, "Sorry, but I don't speak to strangers!" However, the wolf, who had also seen the nightly news, realized where Rhett was going after noticing the contents of her basket. He decided to pay Grandma a visit first.

When the wolf arrived, he heard Grandma singing (somewhat off-key) in her hot tub. He quickly locked the door to that room and put on a very frumpy housedress that was hanging on a nearby hook. He turned the lights down very low.

Soon little Rhett knocked, opened the door, and called to Grandma. The disguised wolf responded weakly, "C'mon into the bedroom, dear." Then they began that famous conversation.

Little did the wolf know, but when Grandma realized what was happening, she picked the lock and came rolling into the bedroom wearing her

Little Rhett Riding's Hood (cont.)

lucky red, white, and blue swimsuit and skates. She carried a camera, flashed it in the wolf's face, and temporarily blinded him.

"Wait until your friends see you in that old housedress!" she laughed as she waited for the picture to develop.

Little Rhett Riding immediately flung off her red cape and twirled it around the wolf, securely tying both ends together. Grandma and little Rhett rolled the wolf out the door and had a very nice afternoon visit.

Read the story's summary below. Cross off any sentences that contain incorrect details.

Grandma hurt herself while in-line skating. She was badly injured and went to the hospital. Her granddaughter, Rhett, saw the incident on television. She decided to bring her a book called *Tips for Safe Roller-Blading*. She packed a basket of items for Grandma, put on her red cape, and left.

While walking, Little Rhett met a very nosey wolf. The wolf, too, had seen the news and wanted to cheer up Grandma.

The wolf arrived first at Grandma's. He gave her a card and some flowers.

He locked Grandma in a room and put on her dress.

Then Rhett arrived at the house. The wolf (disguised as Grandma) invited her inside, and they began to converse.

Meanwhile, Grandma foiled the wolf's plan by calling 911. Grandma escaped, skated into the room, and took a very embarrassing photo of the wolf. Finally, Grandma and Rhett tied the wolf in Rhett's cape and rolled him out the door. Grandma discussed her plans to try sky-diving. Then they had a very pleasant afternoon.

A Neat Nightmare

Heard not a peep, fell right to sleep,
Began to count some woolly sheep.
When suddenly below my bed,
The leader of the monsters said,
"We've lots and lots of work to do.
It will be dawn before we're through!"

Scores of tiny creatures appeared,
Looking up at me, each one sneered.
I pulled the covers close to my head
And watched them work
(while safe in bed).
All my clothes strewn over the floor
Were then thrown down a small, secret
        door.

A twirl of dust swirled all around.
It picked most everything off the
        ground:
Cards, balls, and wooden bats,
Electric toys, and baseball hats.
Gum wrappers, a piece of birthday
        cake,
My favorite, rubber rattlesnake!

It swirled around before my eyes
Then quickly dropped, met its demise
In a machine that chews up things
That fall into its openings.
The monsters cheered with each loud
        "crunch."
They love to hear junk scrunch,
        scrunch!

I looked around. The floor was clean.
All due to that big crunch machine.
My stuff was gone! My room was
        stark!
Two feet appeared then in the dark.
A shadow emerged on the wall.
It nodded at the overhaul.

A voice bellowed, "Good job, well
        done!
I'll recommend you to anyone
Whose child leaves a mess at night.
Then he will store things out of sight!"
She paid the monsters one by one.
At my expense they had their fun!

A Neat Nightmare (cont.)

> Complete the summary by using the phrases in the box.

Phrase Bank

paid them	cleaning the room
twirl of dust	sleeping soundly
was almost bare	mom entered
monsters appeared	down a secret door

A boy was _____ when suddenly, many

_____ and began _____. They

threw mislaid clothing _____. A _____

dropped many of the boy's belongings into a machine that chewed them up. The floor

_____. Then the boy's _____,

thanked the cleaning monsters, and _____.

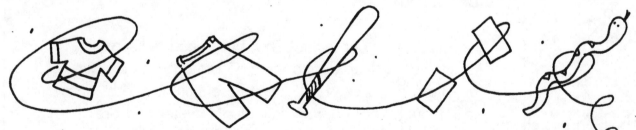

> **Try This:** Recopy the summary, but now fill in the blanks with your own words or phrases. Be creative, but be sure the paragraph makes sense.

Fangs a Lot!

Read the letters, then complete the exercises on page 23.

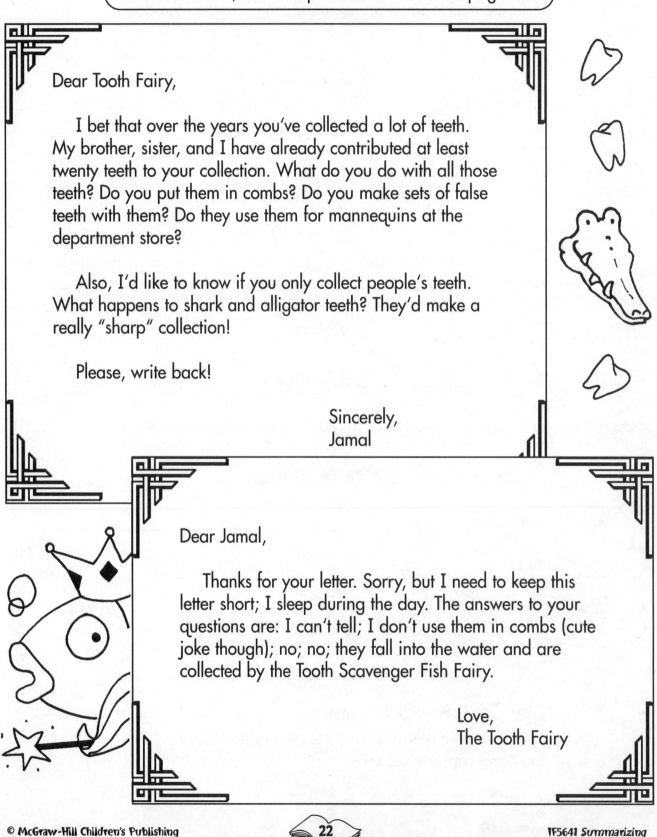

Dear Tooth Fairy,

   I bet that over the years you've collected a lot of teeth. My brother, sister, and I have already contributed at least twenty teeth to your collection. What do you do with all those teeth? Do you put them in combs? Do you make sets of false teeth with them? Do they use them for mannequins at the department store?

   Also, I'd like to know if you only collect people's teeth. What happens to shark and alligator teeth? They'd make a really "sharp" collection!

   Please, write back!

                                        Sincerely,
                                        Jamal

Dear Jamal,

   Thanks for your letter. Sorry, but I need to keep this letter short; I sleep during the day. The answers to your questions are: I can't tell; I don't use them in combs (cute joke though); no; no; they fall into the water and are collected by the Tooth Scavenger Fish Fairy.

                                        Love,
                                        The Tooth Fairy

Name _____

Fangs a Lot! (cont.)

Circle the best ending to each letter's brief summary.

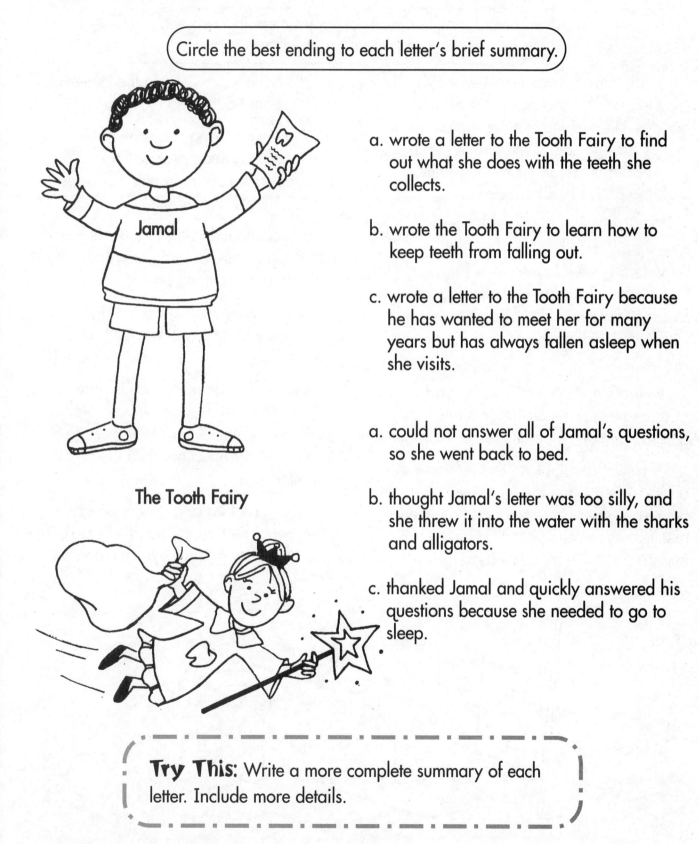

Jamal

The Tooth Fairy

a. wrote a letter to the Tooth Fairy to find out what she does with the teeth she collects.

b. wrote the Tooth Fairy to learn how to keep teeth from falling out.

c. wrote a letter to the Tooth Fairy because he has wanted to meet her for many years but has always fallen asleep when she visits.

a. could not answer all of Jamal's questions, so she went back to bed.

b. thought Jamal's letter was too silly, and she threw it into the water with the sharks and alligators.

c. thanked Jamal and quickly answered his questions because she needed to go to sleep.

Try This: Write a more complete summary of each letter. Include more details.

Growing Up

As you read, notice details of Joey's cleaning project.
Then complete the summary.

By the time he was nine years old, Joey thought he had outgrown most of his toys. He decided to sell them at his mom's garage sale. With that in mind, Joey started to clean his room, rummaging through his bedroom closet.

"I remember this old truck," he thought to himself. "Grandpa and Grandma gave it to me when I turned five. I think Grandpa had as much fun as I did using it to dump sand in the sandbox. It got a little rusty, but it always worked fine."

Joey put the truck into a bag and pushed aside some clothes. He uncovered a shiny, blue and white yo-yo.

"I remember thinking this yo-yo was broken when I first tried it," Joey recalled. "Then I practiced and realized nothing was wrong with it. I even impressed Josh with a few tricks!"

Little by little, the bag in the center of the bedroom floor began to fill up.

"Wow! This brings back memories." Joey held up a neon orange Frisbee. "Last year, my cousins couldn't believe how far I could throw this."

Joey continued to find treasures—an autographed baseball, an old Monopoly game, a small football.

Finally, at the very bottom of the closet, there lay his well-worn teddy bear, Herbie.

"I know I'm definitely too mature for this!" Joey announced to himself. "Teddy bears are for little kids." Joey picked up Herbie and dropped him into the bag of unwanted toys.

Joey leaned up against the bed to survey what he had collected. He looked inside the bag, and his eyes focused on Herbie.

Growing Up (cont.)

"Herbie and I had a lot of fun together," Joey recalled. "I remember when Dad, Mom, and Josh brought him to the hospital when I had my tonsils removed. My throat was sore, and I was so scared. And Herbie sure knew how to make me feel better during storms. When lightning and thunder would wake me up, Herbie and I would pull the covers over our heads, and I would hug him so he wouldn't be scared."

Joey gazed at Herbie one more time and then began thinking about other items in the bag.

"Actually, maybe I'm not too old for these things. After all, they're still in pretty good shape!"

He carried the bag to his closet, dumped its contents in the back, and then grabbed the yo-yo.

"Hey, Josh!" he called to his older brother. "Let's play with my yo-yo. Maybe I can teach you a few new tricks."

Write a word or words on each line that will correctly complete a summary of the story.

Joey felt that he was too _____ for most of his toys and decided to

_____ them. He began to _____ his closet. First, Joey found an old

_____ that his _____ had given him. Next, he discovered a

_____ that he had thought was _____ until he practiced using

it. Then he uncovered a neon _____. Finally, Joey pulled out an old

_____ that had been his best _____ on many occasions. After

_____ about the situation, Joey decided to _____ his old toys

for a while because maybe he wasn't too _____ for them after all.

Say, "Cheese!"

"Everyone, please get into a straight line and listen carefully," announced Mrs. Martinez as she nudged Jack and Parker into line.

"I will give each person a new comb," said the photographer's assistant. "Please do not share."

As soon as she received her comb, Rosa began to comb her long, brown hair down over her eyes. "Help me!" she exclaimed. "My face has disappeared!"

"That's the best you've ever looked," stated Ethan, trying to keep from giggling.

Mrs. Martinez appeared beside the two children. "Rosa and Ethan, go to the end of the line. Rosa, comb your hair the way you usually wear it."

Meanwhile, Trevor whispered to Carlo, "Did you notice how my hair spikes up so straight? The secret is suntan oil. I took a handful and used it this morning. Neat idea, huh?"

Brittany answered, "Cool! Can I touch it?" Trevor nodded, and Brittany started bouncing her hand on his head.

"Brittany, don't touch Trevor's hair!" scolded Mrs. Martinez. Brittany removed her now-greasy hand from Trevor's head and wiped it on the back of Tamara's pink dress.

"Mrs. Martinez!" screeched Tamara. "Brittany just wiped her hand on my favorite dress!"

Mrs. Martinez pointed to the back of the line. "Go!" she commanded.

Meanwhile, Mr. Jacobs, the photographer, began to seat each child one-by-one on a stool. Noah Anderson, the smallest person in the class, sat down.

"You're a little guy, aren't you," observed Mr. Jacobs as he began to raise Noah's seat.

Noah cried, "I can't help it if I'm short!"

"It's special to be short," said Mr. Jacobs, trying to calm Noah down. "Lots of famous people are short."

"Yeah, like that famous mouse in Florida!" teased Wilbur. "You really look like him, especially around the ears!"

Say, Cheese! (cont.)

Noah wailed even louder. Mrs. Martinez sped over to Wilbur and pointed her famous "go to the end of the line" finger. After another minute of consoling and convincing Noah that he really was adorable, Mr. Jacobs took his picture.

"Okay, next," announced Mr. Jacobs, glancing at the large clock on the wall. As Sierra plopped herself down on the stool, scowling at the camera, Mr. Jacobs quietly sighed and muttered to himself, "I knew this was going to be a long day."

Write the story's summary by numbering the following sentences in the correct order. Then recopy them in that order on the back of this paper.

_____ Rosa covered her face with her long hair and was sent to the back of the line.

_____ A tired Mr. Jacobs attempted to photograph a scowling Sierra.

_____ Brittany touched Trevor's spiked hair, wiped her greasy hand on Tamara's dress, and got sent to the end of the line.

_____ The teacher had her class stand in a straight line as they prepared to have their school pictures taken.

_____ Trevor revealed the secret of his spiked hair to Carlo.

_____ Noah cried when he thought Mr. Jacobs was teasing him about being short.

_____ The photographer's assistant distributed combs to the children.

_____ Wilbur teased Noah and got sent to the end of the line.

The Sixth Sense

My teacher seems to know what I'm going to do even before I do it. I remember the time my friend Franco and I decided to sneak back into the coat room. We were going to hide one of every girls' mittens. We had planned our strategy carefully. He'd put some mittens behind the large bookcase, and I'd hide some inside the art storage box that we only open on Fridays.

Suddenly, Mrs. Kracklin appeared in the coat room, smiling that all-knowing smile, and said, "I just know, Chuckie, that you aren't going to touch anyone's clothing. Am I correct, dear?" I nodded and went back to my seat. Franco was laughing.

Another time, I brought my whoopee cushion to school. I really could feel in my bones that this would be a success! I tiptoed to Mrs. Kracklin's desk while she stepped out into the hall. The suspense grew as I waited for her to return.

Without warning, Mrs. Kracklin put her head inside the classroom and announced, "Charles!" (I always get worried when she calls me Charles.) "I would like you to be in charge while I finish talking to Mrs. Greenwood. Please sit at my desk."

"Oh, no!" I thought, mouthing the words. I began to sweat. I slowly approached her desk. I tried to sit as carefully as possible, but it didn't help. Soon everyone was laughing, and I was on my way to the principal's office.

It is just amazing how my teacher senses when I'm going to misbehave. Just like Franco says, she was born with a special gift—a sixth sense.

I'm beginning to believe that Shania Warner is destined to become a teacher, too. She always seems to know when I'm about to play a prank on her. Yesterday, I brought a small, green snake to school. I slid the box onto her desk, but she immediately brought it up to Mrs. Kracklin and said, "Chuckie brought you a present, but he's too shy to give it to you!"

Needless to say, Mr. Marcus, the principal, and I are really getting to know each other.

The Sixth Sense (cont.)

Create a summary. Write the following sentences beside the correct category below.

a. Chuckie tries to fool the teacher into sitting on a whoopee cushion but ends up using it himself.

b. Teachers and future teachers must have a sixth sense.

c. Shania turns the tables and gets Chuckie sent to the office for bringing a snake to school.

d. Chuckie likes to play pranks, but his teacher always seems to discover his plans.

e. Chuckie and his friend attempt to hide the girls' mittens, but Mrs. Kracklin catches them before it happens.

1. Introduction _____

_____

2. First Incident _____

_____

3. Second Incident _____

_____

4. Third Incident _____

_____

5. Conclusion _____

_____

It's What!?!?

Read about an interesting day during summer vacation.

Last Friday began as any other normal day during summer vacation. My little sister Makayla and I scrambled out of bed, got dressed, and quickly consumed bowls of cereal and glasses of orange juice. We darted out the door.

The first thing we did was bounce on our new trampoline. Makayla and I have both improved. We are learning to perfect our knee drops. The seat drops came sort of naturally.

Soon we lost interest and decided to in-line skate. We strapped on our helmets—mine is an awesome purple and Makayla's is electric green. Then we fastened our elbow and knee pads and tightened the buckles on our blades. I called out, "Let's roll!" as several neighbors joined us, and we pretended we were in a roller derby. Eventually, boredom struck, and we once again decided to shift gears and do something different.

Hopscotch sounded fun, so we gathered colored chalk and started to play. After my little sister proved victorious in three games straight, my friend Sally and I talked about what to do next.

The three of us tried jumping rope, but Makayla kept missing and complained that I wasn't twirling the rope correctly. We hung the jump rope on a hook in the garage and finally plopped down on the front porch steps.

"Summer is so-o-o-o-o boring," I announced quite wearily.

"There is never anything fun to do," Makayla added.

Sally nodded in agreement, but soon realized that it was time to return home for lunch.

"We'd better go inside and see what Mom's made for our lunch," I

It's What!?!?! (cont.)

declared. We ran to the kitchen.

"Mom, what's for lunch?" inquired Makayla, sniffing around the room for a clue.

Mom answered, "It's macaroni and cheese and little franks. I decided to make your favorite lunch because you know what happens next week."

"Huh?" I groggily replied, scratching my head. "What's happening next week?"

"School begins on Monday," reminded Mom.

Makayla and I froze in our tracks.

"But, Mom," I whined. "There's so much more we have left to do this summer!"

Makayla and I looked at each other. Reality set in.

Read the following summary of the story. Draw a line through any sentences that may be interesting but are not needed to retell the story.

Last Friday, my sister Makayla and I woke and got ready to play. We ate our favorite energy-boosting breakfast.

The first thing we did was jump on the trampoline. We jumped exceedingly high and improved our drops.

When that became boring, we gathered some neighbors and began to in-line skate. It's fun to pretend we're competing in a roller derby. I just love to "lead the pack" around the block.

Next, we chose to hopscotch. This is Makayla's favorite activity, because she always seems to win. I lost interest quickly, because I always seem to lose.

Maybe a lucky rock would help me.

Once again, we became bored, so we sat on the front porch. Soon it was time for lunch.

Our friend Sally went home, and we walked into our kitchen. Mom had made our favorite meal. I could eat macaroni and cheese with little franks almost any time. Makayla loves it, too.

Then Mom announced that school begins next week. Thoughts of all we had left to do during our vacation floated through our minds.

31

No Girls Allowed!

"Why won't you let us join your club?" Emily yelled up to her brother Eric.

"This club is for boys only!" he answered.

"Besides, girls are so afraid of everything! All we'd hear from you girls is 'Yuck! Bugs!'" added Simon. "You're afraid of even the smallest things!"

"You boys really don't understand girls. You're not as smart as you seem to think!" exclaimed Maggie.

"Oh, let's get out of here! We can play at my house where *boys* aren't allowed," decided Peyton. So the girls scampered off to her house while the boys continued their meeting in the clubhouse.

After arriving at her house, Peyton announced, "I am sick and tired of those boys acting like we can't do the same things they do."

"I've been thinking about that, and I have a plan," announced Maggie. She explained her idea to the other girls and they giggled as they nodded in agreement.

Soon the girls were very busy collecting an assortment of things including flashlights, an old tape recorder, buttons, and pipe cleaners.

The girls worked on their secret project the entire afternoon.

The boys' meeting lasted until dinner. They went home but returned to play baseball.

"See you tomorrow," uttered Eric at seven o'clock as Brandon and Simon headed home.

Later, Eric was climbing into his bed when he heard some noises outside. He noticed a strange light coming from the clubhouse in his yard. "What is that?" he asked aloud. He approached the window to get a closer look and couldn't believe what he saw! Immediately, he called Brandon and Simon on the phone.

"Look outside at our clubhouse! You won't believe it!" he exclaimed breathlessly.

All three boys stared in disbelief. Large creatures with glowing eyes

No Girls Allowed! (cont.)

seemed to cover their clubhouse. Bizarre moans and groans came from inside its walls. The boys knew they'd have to wait until morning to unravel the mystery. So they each lay in bed that night with eyes wide open for hours.

The next morning, the three boys met at the bottom of the oak tree.

"We'd better climb up and see if whatever was in our clubhouse last night is gone today," announced Eric.

"You'd better go up first, Brandon," decided Simon. "You're the club president."

Slowly, each boy climbed the wooden steps to their clubhouse. They

looked at all the strange creatures still hanging around, and began to laugh. Then they saw a note tacked to the wall. It read:

> ### So who's afraid of the big, bad bugs now?
>
> signed,
> The Big, Bad Girls

The boys looked at each other, and Brandon announced, "Okay, they can join. But they'll have to help us clean and 'de-bug' the place first." The two other boys nodded in agreement.

Complete the summary by adding phrases that help retell the story in a brief but complete manner.

The boys and girls were arguing about _____. The girls

decided to _____. Just as the boys were about to

go to sleep, the boys saw _____ and heard

_____ coming from _____. The next morning,

the boys returned to their clubhouse and found _____.

They now realized that the girls _____. So the boys decided

_____.

Football Frenzy

One afternoon, a group of alien children were playing a game of football.

"We must be the toughest, roughest players, not only on Oze, but in the entire Universe!" boasted Ramboze, the team captain.

His friend Herculoze agreed. "I bet we could challenge anyone and easily win!"

Swiftoze added, "And we are the quickest team anywhere in the galaxy!"

Finally, their quarter-back Spideroze hushed his teammates. "C'mon guys, let's prove it! Let's form a traveling team and challenge others in the cosmos so that we can truly claim the title!"

Everyone agreed that this was a fantastic idea. So they packed their uniforms, attached language decoders to their necks, climbed into their mini-spaceship, and began their journey.

On planet after planet, the Ozens easily beat each team.

"This is so easy!" bragged Turboze, their leading fullback.

"The next planet, Earth, should be a real pushover, too!" announced Ramboze. "I predict victory by at least a hundred points!"

Their spaceship traveled through space until it landed in a park directly behind Pee Wee Parker's backyard. Pee Wee and his friends were playing football a few yards away. They froze where they stood and stared in shock as they realized an alien spaceship had just landed.

A loud voice announced, "We have come to your planet in peace. We would like to challenge you to a friendly game of football."

Pee Wee and his friends looked at one another. "Why would they want to play us?" asked Tiny. "We're the scrawniest team in the city."

"We'd better play," decided Melvin. "Otherwise, they might put us in alien stew or something!"

Everyone agreed, but when the gigantic alien team exited their spaceship, the Earthlings gulped in fear.

The players moved to their places on the field. The Ozens' steps seemed to thunder as they slowly crossed the grass.

Football Frenzy (cont.)

"This may not be very pretty to watch," groaned Pee Wee as the first whistle blew.

Suddenly, the boys noticed something interesting. The aliens could barely take a step! Every movement was made in slow motion! Earth was the first planet that the Ozens had visited whose gravity was much greater than their own. Pee Wee's team knew that this was their advantage.

"We may be small, but we can move like lightning compared to them! We'll

be okay as long as we avoid contact!" announced Little Moose in the first huddle.

Their evaluation proved correct. The Mighty Mosquitoes "stung" the Ozens by 36 points!

After their defeat, the Ozen team decided to end their tour of the universe and play for fun in their own backyards.

"There's no place like home!" admitted Ramboze.

Complete the story's summary by circling each correct word or phrase.

Some alien _____ (monsters / children) from the planet Oze were _____ (playing football / eating candy). After continuous _____ (bragging / laughing), the team decided to _____ (read books / challenge teams). They climbed on their spaceship _____ (their spaceship / a shelf) and traveled to many other _____ (stores / planets). Each time the Ozens were _____ (winners / losers). Finally, they arrived on _____ (Earth / Jupiter). They set their ship down on _____ (water / a playground). Then they _____ (challenged / ate) Pee Wee's team. The Mighty Mosquitoes from _____ (Earth / the swamp) proved victorious. The Ozens had difficulty moving quickly because of _____ (gravity / the weather). Eventually, the Ozens flew _____ (kites / home).

My First Job
Part One

As you read, pay close attention to the main characters.

Mrs. Bradford smiled broadly as she let me in the house. "Cassie, you don't realize how grateful Mr. Bradford and I are to see you! We were afraid we wouldn't be able to get a babysitter on such short notice. We will be home about midnight. Here's a list of instructions and an emergency number to call if necessary."

"Bye, Bart!" Mr. and Mrs Bradford both said. "Be sure to listen to Cassie!" They kissed him on the cheek and left.

After they left, I read Mrs. Bradford's note. It said:

> Cassie,
>
> 1. Warm spaghetti in the microwave and feed Bart.
>
> 2. Give Bart a bath and put on his pajamas.
>
> 3. Play a game with Bart.
>
> 4. Put Bart to bed.
>
> 5. Relax and watch television until we return.
>
> In case of emergency, please call 838-3083.

"Simple enough," I thought as I put the note down and headed for the kitchen to feed Bart.

I found the spaghetti in the refrigerator. As I placed the container in the microwave, little Bart stood in front of the open refrigerator and put his hands in a bowl of chocolate pudding.

"No, Bart!" I said firmly as I pulled him away.

"Cassie want some?" Bart asked as he laid his hands on my mouth and all across my face.

I quickly wiped his hands and my face and lowered him into his chair. After heating the spaghetti, I began to feed him dinner.

"No spaghetti!" Bart screeched defiantly. "Gimme a hot dog!"

"Sorry, Bart," I apologized, "but ..." Before I could finish, Bart

IF5641 Summarizing

My First Job—Part One (cont.)

threw the bowl of spaghetti at my head and jumped down onto the floor.

"Bart! Come back!" I yelled as I chased him into the living room, leaving a trail of spaghetti as I went. I finally caught him at the piano rubbing his hands across the keys, and I carried him back to the kitchen and

made him eat the little bit of spaghetti that remained in the bowl. Then I checked the first item off Mrs. Bradford's list.

Next on the list was Bart's bath. He certainly needed one. This time I wasn't going to let him out of my sight.

1. Briefly describe Cassie. _____

_____

_____

2. Briefly describe Bart. _____

_____

_____

3. Write a brief summary of the three ways in which Bart created mischief for Cassie.

   a. _____

   b. _____

   c. _____

  IF5641 Summarizing

My First Job
Part Two

I carried Bart while I got a towel and his pajamas. I even held him while I ran the bath water, making sure that the temperature was perfect. I poured a small amount of bubble bath into the tub. As I lowered Bart slowly into the water, he grabbed the bubble bath and dumped the whole thing into the tub!

"Oh, well," I thought. "At least he'll get really clean."

Soon, bubbles were everywhere! Bart splashed and splashed until every surface was wet. Finally, I rinsed Bart off, dried him, and with some effort, put on his pajamas. I checked off the second item on my list.

"Hmmm," I muttered as I checked the list again. "What kind of game should we play?"

"Cassie build a house!" Bart shouted as I dodged flying building blocks.

"Okay, Bart," I agreed, "but you have to sit perfectly still!" I was surprised that he listened as I built four walls around him.

"This was pretty easy," I thought.

But I had spoken too soon. Bart suddenly stood up and kicked his legs at the blocks, sending them all flying around the room.

I groaned as I checked item number three from my list and said, "It's time for bed."

That announcement triggered a running marathon all through the house until I cornered Bart in the living room closet. I carried him up to his bedroom, and amazingly, he fell asleep almost immediately.

I cleaned and cleaned until the house was immaculate. I turned on the television, plopped exhausted on the couch, and heard the door slowly open.

"Cassie, we're back," said Mr. Bradford in a hushed voice.

"The house looks great!" said Mrs. Bradford. "By the way, we would like to know if you can come back again tomorrow."

"Uh ... I don't think so, Mrs. Bradford. I'm pretty busy until next year—I mean next week."

While I lay in bed that night, I kept thinking that maybe someone had reversed a couple of letters in Bart's name.

My First Job—Part Two (cont.)

1. Briefly describe two times that Bart created mischief for Cassie.

a. _____

_____

b. _____

_____

2. Here is Mrs. Bradford's list of jobs for Cassie. Number the jobs in the order of their occurrence.

_____ Put Bart to bed.

_____ Give Bart a bath.

_____ Warm spaghetti and feed Bart.

_____ Relax. Watch television until we return.

_____ Play a game or play with toys.

Try This: Write a list of helpful tips for babysitters.

Frank & Beanie

My family was the first to arrive at Uncle Frank and Aunt Beanie's annual family barbeque, so we helped get everything ready. Uncle Frank asked me to set up the lawn chairs. As I was putting them around the lawn and pool, Uncle Frank said, "Set that bright orange chair on the line directly in front of the pool. Sit down and push the green button on the armrest as soon as you are comfortable."

I did as I was told. As I sat in the chair, I pushed the button. It began to softly vibrate. Then I started bouncing up and down in my seat. All of a sudden, the chair's seat popped up and gently flung me into the pool! When I came out of the water, I was laughing uncontrollably. It was another of Uncle Frank's fantastic inventions.

After I dried off, Aunt Beanie called for me to help her in the kitchen. I wrapped a towel around my waist and ran inside. "Do you want to see Uncle Frank's latest creation?" she asked me. I nodded.

She led me to what appeared to be a tiny roller coaster sitting on the kitchen table.

"This isn't a toy if that's what you're thinking," she said. "It's Uncle Frank's *Savor the Flavor—Roller Coaster Condiments Machine*. Let's try it."

Aunt Beanie placed a hot dog in a bun and put it inside a car on the coaster. "Let's see," she said as she began pushing some buttons. "This hot dog needs the works!" Slowly, the car went down the tracks. After it climbed the first hill, bright red ketchup squirted. Spicy mustard sprayed out of a nozzle at the first curve. As the hot dog raced down the hill, onions dropped from a mini-umbrella. At the next curve, relish was added, and finally, a slice of cheese was placed on top by small, mechanical hands.

"Wow!" I exclaimed. "Everyone will love it!"

And love it, they did! Everyone ate extra hot dogs just so they could try the machine again. Then afterwards, they took turns on Uncle Frank's special lawn chair!

Frank and Beanie (cont.)

Complete the summary by adding phrases that help retell the story in a brief but complete manner.

1. Today, the speaker is excited because _____

_____.

2. The speaker is helping _____.

3. Uncle Frank first asks the speaker to _____

_____.

4. The speaker is quite surprised when _____

_____.

5. Next, Aunt Beanie directs the speaker to _____

_____.

6. There, Aunt Beanie demonstrates _____

_____.

7. After the demonstration, the speaker _____

_____.

Try This: Describe what you think Uncle Frank might invent for next year's barbeque. Draw and label a diagram of the invention.

T.V. Troubles

My friend Raan has a vivid imagination. He probably gets it from watching so much television. Raan is especially fond of cartoons and can watch them for hours. And it really doesn't matter how many times he's seen the same cartoon. This is why we refer to him as "Rerun."

Rerun loves to relate his cartoon adventures. Sometimes, he believes these fictional characters actually exist.

"Get real!" we'll exclaim as Rerun tells us how a coyote chased him and his roadrunner friend through the desert.

"This *is* real!" he'll say back as he finishes the story.

Then a little later, Rerun will relate a "true" experience he had with a panther detective, who just happened to be pink.

On one particular morning, Rerun came racing toward a group of us, brimming with the details of his latest cartoon exploit.

"Sit down!" he loudly announced. "Even I would have trouble believing what I am about to say!" So we plopped down and got comfortable. We knew this was going to be a whopper!

Rerun began, "Last night, I was watching an episode of *Chick'n Lick'n*. Chick'n was marching around the henhouse, guarding the hens from mischief.

"Suddenly, a huge net fell down over Chick'n. Foxy Roxy called out, 'I'd like to invite you for a fried chicken dinner with all of the trimmings, but I can see that you are all tied up!' Chick'n could hear Foxy snickering as she disappeared into the henhouse.

"No matter how hard he tried, Chick'n couldn't escape the net. It broke my heart to think what might happen to those hens inside! So I walked up to the television and touched the screen. Suddenly, I could feel Chick'n's wing actually pulling me inside the T.V. When I stopped moving, I noticed that an amazing transformation had occurred. I had turned into a chicken!

T. V. Troubles (cont.)

"'What happened?' I asked Chick'n as my beak fell wide open.

"'I can't explain now. My girls and I need your help!,' Chick'n pleaded. 'Slip inside the henhouse and help them before that fox causes them harm!'

"So I tiptoed inside. Foxy had tied up the hens and had placed them inside a wagon that she was beginning to pull through the door. Wasting no time, I rolled a rock under each front wheel, causing the wagon to abruptly stop. The hens squawked, and the fox looked perplexed. She peered under the wagon, and that's when I let her have it! I threw some hay at her face, which temporarily blinded her. Then I dropped an egg basket over her head.

"Quickly, I released the chickens from the wagon, picked up a rake, and knocked Foxy into the wagon. I removed the rocks bracing the wheels, and the hens and I pushed the wagon with all of our might. It rolled until it was completely out of sight.

"Finally, we lifted the net from Chick'n, and everyone peeped with delight. Chick'n thanked me, and suddenly I found myself sitting back on the living room couch."

We all smiled at Rerun's story, doubting its contents until Rerun adjusted his baseball cap and a few feathers fell gently to the ground.

Use another sheet of paper to write a summary of the story. Retell the story concisely, leaving out unnecessary details.

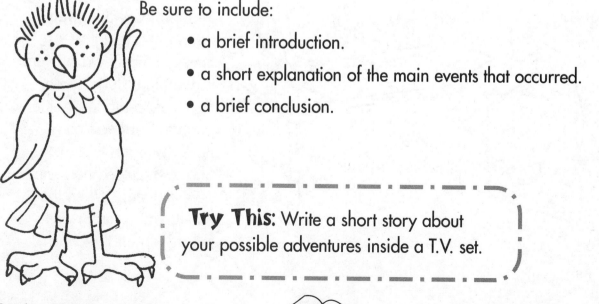

Be sure to include:

- a brief introduction.
- a short explanation of the main events that occurred.
- a brief conclusion.

Try This: Write a short story about your possible adventures inside a T.V. set.

Choices

"Mom, let's watch a video tonight," suggested Brianna, "and have popcorn, too."

"I can pop some popcorn," agreed her mom, "but I've got lots of work to do. I'll have to pass on the video."

Brianna's mom popped the popcorn and placed it on the coffee table near the television. Brianna carried in a bottle of soda pop and set it nearby.

"Let's see," said her mom. "Here is a cute movie about a clown. It's called *Clowning Around*. You'll love it."

She put the video into the VCR and left to finish her work at the computer.

Brianna got comfortable on the

sofa, and began to watch the clown. She saw the clown squirt his flower at another clown. She listened to him tell jokes and observed him playing tricks on unsuspecting victims. Finally, she decided that the clown was funny, but she was tired of watching one silly clown act after another.

Brianna walked over to the cabinet where they kept their videos and decided to find something a little more interesting.

"Hmm . . . *Super Duck, Digger the Dog* . . ." she read through the film titles, "I've seen these a million times. There's got to be something better.

Finally, Brianna smiled broadly. *King Kong*! she exclaimed. "Mom says I'm too young to see this, but how scary can one monkey be?"

So Brianna put *King Kong* into the VCR. She even turned off the lights. At first, the movie wasn't very frightening. But as King Kong began to terrify the people, Brianna's confidence began to waver. She even closed her eyes several times. When the movie was over, Brianna fell asleep on the couch,

Choices (cont.)

clutching her pillow.

After a while, Brianna's mom walked into the family room and woke her. Brianna jumped up, a look of fear on her face.

"Mom," she exclaimed. "I just had the worst nightmare! A gigantic clown was climbing the Empire State Building! He thought it was funny to catch planes and fling them in all directions! He even squirted a huge flower at a passing helicopter!"

"Honey," her mother responded, trying to calm her, "it was only a bad dream. I bet eating all that popcorn before falling asleep caused it."

Her mother got up and took the tape out of the VCR.

"Or, maybe it was making a bad choice," concluded Brianna's mother.

Write a summary of the story. Retell the story concisely, leaving out unnecessary details. Be sure to include:

- a brief introduction.

- a short explanation of the main events that occurred.

- a brief conclusion.

_____

_____

_____

_____

_____

_____

_____

Answer Key

Clever Boy, Wise Mom 4

4, 2, 1, 2, 6, 5, 2, 3, 5

"Chews"ing a Dentist 5

zookeeper, dentist, friend, cleaned, insurance, charges, zookeeper, appointment, zookeeper, alligator, appointment

Harry 6

1. a

2. c

3. b

A Birthday Surprise! 7

Suggested answers:

birthday, son, cake, mess, kitchen, garden, flowers, mother, living room, smiled

The mother would thank the boy then discover the mess in the kitchen.

Mayra's Backpack Attack 8

Mayra, backpack, spelling, frog, beetle, flash, monkey, pen, candy, cookie, gum, sticky, new

Vroo-o-o-m! 9

Suggested answers:

car, steering wheel, tires, wings, water, bridge, Wheels, burn rubber, laughs

Howdy Pahdner! 10

1. c

2. a

3. b

Presto Chango! 11

1. b

A Change in Attitude 12–13

circle the first verse, box the last verse

1. 5, 6, 4, 1, 3, 2

A Surprise Guest 14

circle letter c

A Breakfast of Winners 15

Group 1—underline b

Group 2—underline a

Choosing Friends Wisely 16

cruel, better, confidence, humble

Whodunit? 17

Mom yelled from the kitchen that her cake was half-eaten. I followed cake crumbs from the kitchen to the living room. I carefully checked my dad, little brother, and dog for crumbs. The parrot's cage was open. Pollyanna said, "Aloha," a Hawaiian word. Since pineapples are grown in Hawaii, I concluded that the parrot had eaten the cake.

Little Rhett Riding's Hood 18–19

Cross out the following:

1. She was badly injured and went to the hospital.

2. She decided to bring her a book called *Tips for Safe Blading.*

3. The wolf, too, had seen the news and wanted to cheer up Grandma.

4. He gave her a card and some flowers.

5. Meanwhile, Grandma foiled the wolf's plan by calling 911.

6. Grandma discussed her plans to try sky-diving.

A Neat Nightmare................................**20–21**

sleeping soundly, monsters appeared, cleaning the room, down a secret door, cyclone of dust, was almost bare, mom entered, paid them

Fangs a Lot!................................**22–23**

Jamal—a

The Tooth Fairy—c

Growing Up................................**24–25**

Suggested Answers:

old, sell, look through, truck, grandparents, yo-yo, broken, Frisbee, teddy bear, friend, thinking, keep, old

Say, "Cheese!"................................**26–27**

3, 8, 5, 1, 4, 6, 2, 7

The Sixth Sense................................**28–29**

1. d

2. e

3. a

4. c

5. b

It's What!?!?................................**30–31**

Cross out the following sentences:

1. We ate our favorite energy-boosting breakfast.

2. We jumped exceedingly high and improved in our drops.

3. It's fun to pretend we're competing in a roller derby.

4. I just love to "lead the pack" around the block.

5. This is Makayla's favorite activity because she always seems to win.

6. I lost interest quickly, because I always seem to lose.

7. Maybe a lucky rock would help me.

8. Mom had our favorite meal.

9. I could eat macaroni and cheese with little franks almost any time.

10. Makayla loves it, too.

No Girls Allowed!................................**32–33**

Suggested Answers:

the girls joining the club, play at Peyton's, lights and creatures, weird sounds, their clubhouse, the "bugs" and a note, had played a trick, to let them join

Football Frenzy................................**34–35**

Circle the following:

children, playing football, bragging, challenge teams, their spaceship, planets, winners, Earth, a playground, challenged, Earth, gravity, home

My First Job—Part One................................**36–37**

Answers may vary:

1. Cassie is a young girl on her first babysitting job. She is confident, determined, and a hard worker.

2. Bart is a young and mischievous child who causes trouble for Cassie.

3. a. He put his hand in the chocolate pudding

   b. He throws the spaghetti

   c. tracks spaghetti through the house

My First Job—Part Two......................38–39

1. Answers may vary:

   a. He dumps the bubble bath into the tub.

   b. He kicks blocks all over the room.

2. 4, 2, 1, 5, 3

Frank and Beanie...........................40–41

Suggested Answers:

1. it is the day of the annual family barbecue at Frank and Beanie's.

2. Uncle Frank set up chairs.

3. put chairs around the pool and lawn.

4. a lawn chair he sat in flung him into the pool.

5. help in the kitchen.

6. Uncle Frank's new invention, a condiment-serving machine.

7. was very excited and told everyone about the invention.

T.V. Troubles...............................42–43

Answers will vary. An example is:

   Raan is very interested in television, especially in cartoons. He occasionally tells his friends stories about "adventures" that he has had, based on his favorite cartoon characters. One day, he tells his friends about helping to rescue hens from a villain named Foxy Roxy. To do the rescuing, he is transported into the T.V. and changed into a chicken. Raan's friends question the truth of the story until chicken feathers fall from his baseball hat.

Choices..................................44–45

Answers will vary. An example is:

   Brianna suggests that she and her mother watch a movie together, but Mother is busy. She chooses an appropriate movie for Brianna. The girl becomes bored and chooses a movie that her mother has previously said may be too scary for her. After watching the movie, Brianna falls asleep, only to have a terrible nightmare.